Lost:
Children of the
River

Edited by Gabriel H. Sanchez

and Isaac Chavarría

I0629595

Cover Art
"De Sur a Norte" by Jose G. Cano

Cover Art Photograph
by Ileana Garcia-Spitz

ISBN: 0692638008
ISBN-13: 978-0692638002

DEDICATION

We would like to dedicate this book to the many people working hard to assist the refugee families coming to the United States from Central America. Special gratitude to Sacred Heart Catholic Church, the Catholic Charities of the Rio Grande Valley, and all the volunteers and donors to that effort.

Our gratitude goes to the persons who helped us raise funds to make this collection a reality. A big thank you as well to the artists, writers, and photographers who contributed to this project.

Lastly, this book is dedicated to the refugee families, especially the little children whose innocence is worth preserving so that as they grow they may remember the many who came together to protect them from the dangers they were facing in their home countries and all along their path to the land of the free.

CONTENTS

Refugees: Hope in an Uncertain Future   ix
By Brenda Riojas

Retando a la Bestia por un Sueño   1
By Isis Hinojosa

Refugees…Not Illegals!!!   3
By Christopher Carmona

Helping with the Refugee Crisis in the Border   6
By Ana M. Fores Tamayo

If I Come To Your Door   20
By PW Covington

Inocencia Interumpida   22
By Raquel López Suárez

In the Dark, Drifting   24
By Octavio Quintanilla

Vigil   25
By Octavio Quintanilla

Unaccompanied Minors   26
By Phyllis Wax

New Shoes   28
By Aida Escalante

New Shoes at IC Cathedral   29
By Aida Escalante

Refugees   30
By Cesar Riojas

Refugees II   31
By Cesar Riojas

Don't Be Afraid Gringo, A Honduran   32
Woman Speaks From the Heart: The Story
of Elvia Alvarado
By Edward Vidaurre

Untamed   33
By Amalia L. Ortiz

Borderland Blood Moon   35
By Cesar D. Leon

Dreaming in Noir: Chapter One Hundred   36
Forty-Five (Para los Niños de la Frontera)
By Fernando Esteban Flores

Which Way's Home   37
By Fernando Esteban Flores

For Gilbert Ramos   39
By Joseph Ross

Pues Lo Que Ha Pasado   41
By Sister Juliana Garcia

Child From Central America   43
By Brenda Riojas

Children Left to Wander   44
By Jenny Campos Galvan

Mother and Son   45
By Brenda Riojas

Welcome Flags   46
By Brenda Riojas

Historia Viviente   47
By Sister Juliana Garcia

Entre Amigos   48
By Brenda Riojas

Aaaayyy! Mis Hijooooooossss!   50
By Nephatlí de León

Children of the River   52
By Nephatlí de León

Untitled   55
By Sister Norma Pimentel

Border Heads   56
By Celeste de Luna

Contributors   57

INTRODUCTION

Refugees: Hope in an Uncertain Future

By Brenda Riojas

Unless the storm hits in our backyard we tend to remain asleep, unaware of the wind force shaking lives miles away, uprooting families, tossing them in different directions.

In the summer of 2014 the world's eyes turned to the U.S./Mexico border; they turned to McAllen, Texas and Reynosa, Mexico. The media streamed in from all directions – *Texas Monthly*, *Time Magazine*, *L.A. Times*, CNN, and the British Broadcasting Corporation (BBC News). Correspondents from Amsterdam, Australia, Japan, Germany, and more came to cover the stories of immigrants arriving from Central America. Reporters wanted to focus on the unaccompanied minors. They wanted to understand how a parent could send their child alone on a dangerous journey into a foreign country. They asked the same questions: "Why did you leave your country? What did you leave behind? What was the journey like? How were you treated along the way? What are your plans here in the United States?"

The storm of violence in Central America forcing people to take refuge elsewhere woke us up to the stories of unaccompanied minors who are in the United States; an influx of unprecedented numbers. From October 1, 2013 to September 30, 2014 more than 68,000 minors crossed the border; it was estimated the number would reach 90,000 by the end of the fiscal year. This is not a new story. Prior to the summer of 2014, there were already four centers in the Rio Grande Valley for unaccompanied minors. Since the influx, the number has increased to 14. Alongside the stories of unaccompanied minors crossing are stories of mothers who come with their children escaping the violence of their homeland in Central America's northern triangle. They travel 10, 15, 20 days (some up to a month or more) to find their way to the United States. They come looking for a safe place to raise their children. The children are not "unaccompanied." Parents are entrusting their child to a friend, neighbor, or relative, who is making the journey in this direction, and most have a family member who is waiting for them in this country: a father, a mother, an aunt, a brother.

In a *Time Magazine* opinion piece, Joe Klein compared the countries they are leaving as the "Latino equivalent of Syria or Iraq." "But in Central America," he adds, "its anarchy, not religious fanaticism, they are fleeing, the rampaging of militant gangs." What would you do if your son was forced to join a gang or face death? If your daughter could be kidnapped at any moment? The countries they flee – Honduras, Guatemala and El Salvador, are the most dangerous in the world. They rank in the top 10 countries with the highest murder rates. Honduras ranks at the top, where the chances of getting murdered are 1 in 14.

"What we are seeing unfold in front of our eyes is a humanitarian and refugee reality, not an immigration problem," writes Bishop Daniel E. Flores in his blog. Embedded in this unfolding are the stories of courageous women of faith; mothers, aunts, even grandmothers are speaking up against the violence in their homelands and speaking through their actions, fleeing what they know in a desperate attempt to protect their families, even if it means facing danger. From Honduras came Maxelina, Rosa Evilinda, Marta; from Guatemala Maria Luisa, Griselda, Hermosinda; from El Salvador Yenny Lezeth, Maria, and thousands more are risking everything, taking desperate measures, selling their homes, asking for loans, crossing into unknown territory with their children in their arms. "Vienen para poder vivir," said Sister Juliana Garcia, a Missionary of Jesus, who visited the respite center established by Catholic Charities of the Rio Grande Valley in McAllen. They come so that they may live. They arrive here on hope and prayers.

More than 68,000 refugees, classified as "family units" by the Department of Homeland Security, have crossed into the United States from October 1, 2013 to September 30, 2014. They have been apprehended, detained and released by U.S. Immigration and Customs Enforcement with instructions to appear in court at a specified date. After their release, their journey continues as they travel to meet with family members scattered throughout the United Sates. Some are traveling north to Boston, Chicago, or New York, and others west to Los Angeles or east to Florida. The refugee women we meet at the parish who share their stories bless us with their determination to persevere, with their resolve to journey ahead even as their future remains uncertain. I admire their courage. They are navigating in a foreign land and facing deportation. Many of them don't even know what they are signing when they are processed through Immigration and Customs

Enforcement. It broke my heart when a woman with two children from El Salvador asked me to explain to her what she had signed. "Por favor explíqueme lo que firme." What she signed were her deportation papers. Her only crime, crossing into the United States illegally. She did not leave her birth city of San Salvador on a whim, seeking riches. She came as a refugee. She, like the thousands who are crossing, took this desperate measure to save her children's lives, to find a safe place to live.

There are some in our country who want the U.S. government to return the women and children to their homelands. While "we are a nation of laws," as Texas Governor Rick Perry said before a U.S. House field hearing in July, we must remember we are also a nation that cares. I have witnessed this caring and the outpouring of help at Sacred Heart Church in McAllen and at Immaculate Conception Cathedral in Brownsville where Catholic Charities of the Rio Grande Valley is providing newly arrived immigrants with some basics needs – food, clothing, a shower, a place to rest and medical attention prior to their continued journey. Caring volunteers have assisted more than 14,000 people since the first respite center opened on June 10 in McAllen.

We applaud as our immigrant brothers and sisters come through the doors of Sacred Heart Church parish hall. We welcome them, the women and children who braved an often dangerous trek from their homelands in Honduras, El Salvador and Guatemala. We cry with them, and we stand in solidarity with their desire for asylum. These women of faith are taking bold moves in their struggle to live. We pray partisan politics will not stand in the way. Pope

Francis also asks, "We pray for a heart which will embrace immigrants. God will judge us on how we have treated the most needy."

The women and children arriving on our border, this gateway to what they consider a safer place, forces us to pay attention, to take action, to help. The current humanitarian challenge is a test of the moral character of our nation. We cannot contribute to what Pope Francis calls a "globalization of indifference." He reminds us in his message for the World Day of Migrants and Refugees, "A change of attitude towards migrants and refugees is needed on the part of everyone, moving away from attitudes of defensiveness and fear, indifference and marginalization – all typical of a throwaway culture – towards attitudes based on a culture of encounter, the only culture capable of building a better, more just and fraternal world".

What we saw this summer is a mere glimpse of men and women who risk everything in an attempt to save their lives, and the lives of their children. The story does not end when the cameras and reporters leave. We continue to meet the refugees and hear their stories daily at Sacred Heart Church at the respite center in McAllen.

Siguen huyendo, siguen llegando, seguimos ayudando.

RETANDO A LA BESTIA POR UN SUEÑO

By Isis Hinojosa

¿Un viaje a los sueños?
o ¿un viaje a una real pesadilla?
En un largo camino del sur a el norte,
seres con un futuro incierto,
rostros curtidos por el dolor,
con los bolsillos casi vacíos
y sus corazones llenos de esperanzas
suben a la bestia. La tristeza, el temor,
el hambre, la sed, la angustia
y todas las esperanzas de llegar
al tan prometido sueño americano
son las emociones y sentimientos
que se transportan en medio de los terribles cambios climáticos.

Sus miradas al cielo buscan consuelo.
Sus pensamientos son como un águila en vuelo
en busca de la libertad, el valor de sus almas
y del honor que se les han arrebatado.
Hombres y mujeres se miran unos a otros,
por sus mentes cruzan los buenos deseos
para un mejor porvenir,
pequeños inocentes viajan sin entender porqué
no pueden jugar mientras se aferran a el ardiente vagón de tren.
La bestia carga en su lomo cientos de vidas a diario, pero no es

gratis,
ella es como una serpiente traicionera
y cobra el viaje con robos, injusticias, violaciones
y muchas veces con la muerte.

Ya casi para cruzar descansan bajo ella
aquellos que lograron llegar a la frontera donde el río les espera...
Algunos logran llegar al otro lado
y si corren con suerte, entonces su pesadilla habrá terminado,
pero si no la migra los ha de regresar
y con ellos sus sueños truncados.
Cuando los veas inclina tu cabeza
y rinde honor a su nobleza, fuerza y valentía.
Ellos no vienen a quitarnos nada,
ellos vienen en busca de trabajo y dignidad.

REFUGEES…NOT ILLEGALS!!!

By Christopher Carmona

clap clap clap

a journey of a thousand steps begins with a single atrocity

gang initiate   kill father/brother/mother   now you are one of us

tattoo name   on face   choices vanished/taken

              like hymens in the desert

random kidnappings   kill kill kill   America needs its drugs

nations destabilized   profit profit profit   only choice

sell everything   for a single hope

clap clap clap

a journey of a single step begins with a thousand atrocities

a thousand guns   a single ignorance   leads to war

against starving children

locked in cages like animals   lights always on   shoe laces taken

always kept cold   kills the smell   no blankets

pesticides keep them warm

dropped at bus station   no belongings   taken by ICE

only papers   that allow   access to country

clap clap clap

a journey of a thousand atrocities begins with a single ignorance

refugees not illegals   fleeing gang war torn country   risked it all

refugees not illegals   rape is imminent   fathers can't protect

refugees not illegals   sons with guns to head husbands can't protect

refugees not illegals   wife/daughter/sister/mother   can't protect

clap clap clap

a journey of a single atrocity begins with a thousand ignorances

guns guns guns   soldiers/fences/national guard

            protect us from sense of safety

patriots patriots patriots bring your guns and your hate

                protect us from the innocent and the desperate

policy policy policy   politicians/pundits/photo ops

            bring teddy bears/soccer balls/and plastic faces

tweet tweet tweet   send them back   they do not belong

                dangerous and diseased

celebrites celebrities celebrities   no one on site just Glenn Beck
            cooking for no refugees

no Sean Penns   no Eva Longorias   no Edward James Olmos'
no George Clooneys

not even an Angelina Jolie   to buy Latino kids

4

to complete her kids from around the world collection

guess, not far enough away   not fashionable enough

to fake concern   to fake volunteer

clap clap clap

a single shower   a hot meal   a new change of clothes

cleanses the soul   like a thousand masses with bent knees   ever

could

priest in detention center prays over children

reminds them/reminds us   they are still human beings

clap clap clap

a thousand hearts   countless hours   no need for compensation

families knowing only cruelty

met with hugs/crayons/and sandwiches

a journey of a single smile begins with a thousand compassions

clap clap clap

***every time a new refugee family walks through the doors
at Sacred Heart (the refugee center in McAllen, TX), all
of the volunteers stop what they are doing and clap
to commemorate their arriving at a safe space***

HELPING WITH THE REFUGEE CRISIS IN THE BORDER

By Ana M. Fores Tamayo

On Friday, August 10th, the day after the Murrieta rally in Austin, my husband Andrés and I went to help the church of Cristo Rey pack up donations for the refugees. We joined a group from the Austin Immigrant Rights Coalition, spending six hours on our feet, sorting and moving clothes and a few toys, so that we could pack up a truck they were renting to take to McAllen, Texas. It was over 100 degrees all day, but luckily, we were not outside that long. I kept thinking about the refugees as they walked and walked in the heat.

The truck was filled top to bottom with donated clothes. So was our Ford Expedition behind it.

The next morning we left Austin at 6 am so that we could get to McAllen's Sacred Heart by noon. When we arrived, volunteers walked us through the process of what they do for the refugee families the border control detention centers let go, so they can stay with relatives while they await their hearing, which concerns "removal proceedings" in immigration court.

Originally —since these centers are so overcrowded— they would let a lot of refugees go, dropping them off at the Greyhound Bus Terminal with no money, no food, dirty and worn from a trip of who knew how long to the north, besides who knew how long of a detention at the center without a shower, even. The good folks of McAllen began to notice, and they would go to help.

First one, then another.

Before they realized it, McAllen and the surrounding county of Hidalgo decided this could not continue, and Catholic charities with other religious and service organizations decided to act. They stepped in to provide shelter for these people before they had to go on their way. Thus they established Sacred Heart as the refugee center: a place for these weary travelers to shower, get fresh clothing with which to change, good home-made food to eat, and a chance to talk to people who would not turn them away, who were sympathetic to their suffering.

"'Taxpayers are paying for it and they are all behind it,' Josh Ramirez said, director of the city agency providing support to the immigrants.

Sister Norma Pimentel and her army of volunteers and donors run the shelter out of a parish hall.

The Rio Grande Valley is one of the poorest regions in the U.S. Yet since the centre opened in early June, residents, businesses and the city have contributed huge amounts of clothing, food, diapers, soaps, medical aid, legal aid and other help " (source: William Mardsen, Canada.com, August 10, 2014).

Refugees travel by whatever means necessary to get to the border, and when they get across, they surrender to Border Patrol. At the detention center, they are held anywhere from a couple of days to as many as five or six, sometimes even more. The refugees with family who will pay for their bus ticket to join them might be released —with nothing but the clothes on their backs and a manila envelope enclosing their immigration papers that affirm stolidly, "Removal Proceedings."

It is at this point that the shelter established only a few blocks from the Greyhound Bus Terminal at Sacred Heart takes them in. All the folks from McAllen have joined in helping these refugees, as they like to call them. It is a humanitarian crisis, they believe, and the people of McAllen are assisting with this need, as one good soul succors another.

The 57,000 unaccompanied children coming across the border are not included in the aid the center gives the children who come with mothers —along with a few fathers as well— though usually men and women are separated at the detention centers. One woman was telling me that she was placed on one side, along with her two children, while she stared at her husband on the other side of a huge room, her heart broken after all they had been through together. She felt that she would eventually be released, yet her husband, who knew? She could only gaze after him, too weary and numb from the journey to even cry.

These are the families Sacred Heart Center supports. Although the organizers have been trying for months to get in to see the unaccompanied children too, they have still not been successful. In the meantime, however, the families they do service are plenty enough. They have assisted over 6000 people already. These young families leave Sacred Heart with full stomachs, clean bodies, at least one set of clothes —besides the change they are wearing— clean shoes, socks, undergarments, and happy knowing that not everyone is like most of the border patrol and other officers they encounter at the detention centers.

New sneakers of all sizes donated by some good Samaritan

With the openhearted folk they meet in the center at *Sacred Heart*, the refugee families realize from that first welcoming clap as they enter the doors of the church that not everyone in the United States wants to place them in crowded cells, with throngs of people swarming about them. The United States is not —unlike what they dreamed— small rooms and stinking toilets reeking next to them, all out in the open for everyone to see. Not all people believe that they deserve so little privacy, that they are worse than animals. They finally get to see the humanity of McAllen, of the United States, and that is a much-appreciated reprieve after all the suffering they have experienced.

So *Sacred Heart Center* has its hands more than full with the families released day and night. Both nights I volunteered to work at the bus station —making sure the mothers with their children got on their right bus— there were at least 30 people each night waiting to take buses to their varied destinations. They were going everywhere each night: from Houston to Miami, to Chicago, to Boston and New York City, to L.A. They were going north, south, east, and west. And we waited with them, during this first part of their American journey, hoping they would not encounter that same type of beast that brought most of them north to the Rio Grande Valley.

I am happy holding a smiling baby at the McAllen Greyhound Bus Station with my husband Andrés L. Pacheco, while the mother went to the restroom before boarding the bus on her long journey to the north.

Folks who are so dead set against helping —against doing anything for these refugees— should only go to work at this center for two to three hours to change their minds. There, they will encounter an incredible system that has been established, in make shift style over the past four months, since June. The city of McAllen, with help from all types of organizations and individuals from all corners, has set up an entire system of doctors and nurses, lawyers, psychological trauma counselors. They have put up makeshift showers at *Sacred Heart,* a food pantry, and tables upon tables filled with clothes of all sizes. Volunteers pack clothes and food for these mothers with children —for their coming trip to their waiting families— so they will not suffer as they did struggling up through Central America and Mexico.

All this is done through a vast and still growing volunteer network, made up of wonderful people who are now coming from every state and even from other countries (a trauma counselor was flying back to Portugal on my 4th day there).

But there is one core group of main volunteers, the ones who live in McAllen, the ones who began the program, the ones who stay there and who go daily —no matter their politics— to lend a helping hand.

Alejandro Cáceres, from Austin Immigrant Rights Coalition, *volunteers for the day at* Sacred Heart Church.

While the families

are showering, the volunteers gather a change of clothes for them, and, depending on how long their trip is, maybe even two or three sets. Sometimes these families have to wade through six or seven different bus tickets before they reach their destination. So mothers are given one change of clothes, older children two sets, while the youngest receive three sets, since they dirty them up the quickest. Imagine all the donations McAllen is receiving, but yet still needs to receive!

Moms need to carry the food and babies, so they get the least clothing so as not to weigh them down. Volunteers put everything in one small backpack —also donated— as they have another pack that the shelter gives them with food for the road. The center has the entire system worked out.

There are volunteers who advise the mothers about their journey; they explain what their bus ride will be like, how many stops they will have to make, and how to get around the different bus stations. They also advise them and tell them what to do if no one speaks Spanish, showing them a readymade document they carry in their paperwork with the words, *"Help me, I do not speak English."* The volunteers let the young mothers call their final destination, so folks on the other side are aware when they will arrive, and these women even get to call home, to Central America, so people there know they are safe and taken care of in a good place.

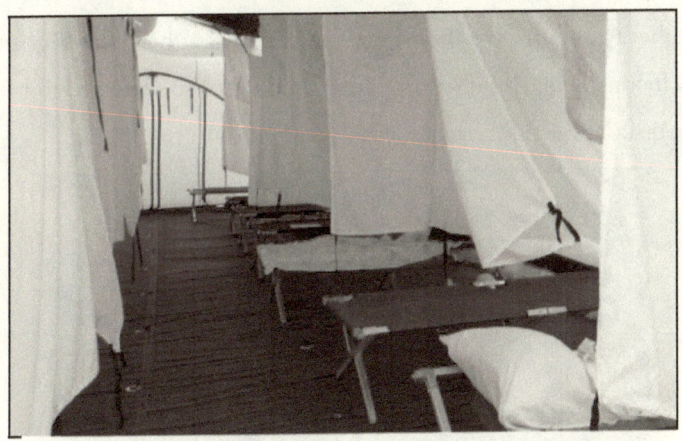

Cots at Sacred Heart Center where refugee families rest after they get ready, before they go to the McAllen Greyhound Bus Terminal, to begin the next part of their journey.

But before arriving at Sacred Heart, the detention center the Border Patrol took refugees to was far from what these families imagined the United States to be. From what these women told me time and time again, the holding cells at the detention center are just like those photographs we have all seen: 60 to 80 people in a freezing room, where they even have to sleep in the bathrooms, on the floor, without anything to cover them in the frigid rooms, *hieleras*, they call them. If they are placed in separate holdings, those look like dog cages, one of the young mothers told me…

This young woman also murmured that the guards took all her baby's clothes away and left him only in diapers, so the baby was shivering, trembling, his lips blue with cold. When she asked for something to cover him, they gave her a thermal blanket, but they did not explain what it was. She had never seen anything like thermal blankets, which look like foil paper. What was the young mother to think; were these Americans mocking her? She began to cry inconsolably, holding on to her child desperately to give him her body's warmth, crying her hot tears into his frosty skin.

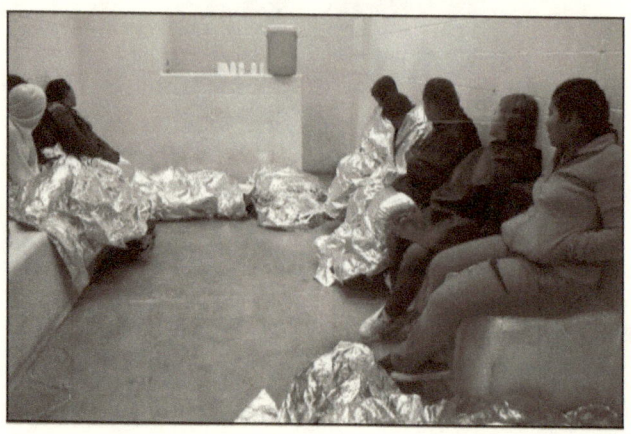

Small holding cell at the deportation centers where refugees are held indefinitely, sometimes as many as 60 – 80 to a room.

(Photo by John Moore/Getty Images)

The young mother continued… the guards did not feed them well at all. She was there for 24 hours or so, and she received one small bottle of water and a tortilla with a little rice and beans. That was it. This mother was nursing. Another nursing mother told me they fed her only apples for two days straight. She thought she would faint. Since this young mother had begun her trip, she had lost 8 pounds and her baby six. On one of the last days I was there, I was taking care of two sisters, a young one and a teenager. They were so happy to be there, to get clean clothes and to eat a decent meal. They drank the soup the volunteers served as if they had never tasted anything so good. Then they went for seconds lickety-split.

When I took the girls to the showers with their change of clothing, they were excited to put on and show off their "new" things. But a few minutes into the shower, the teen called out to me. I came over, and she held out her long thin arm to me, saying that she didn't think she could stand. I glimpsed her falling figure from behind the half open shower door, trying as hard as she could to keep from fainting. She looked at me desperately: "I think I am going to be sick... I am so so sorry..." I told her to throw up right there, not to worry about anything; it was very easy to pick it up from the shower stall. She was ashamed to be sick, yet I knew what was causing it.

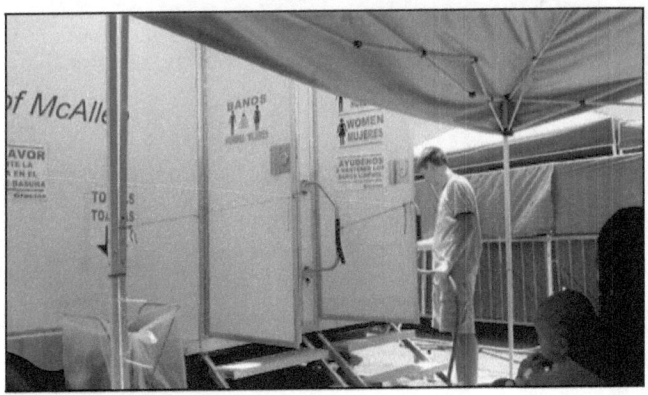

A young monk who came to volunteer for two weeks from the Midwest was scrubbing the makeshift showers, which they clean religiously after each use.

The detention centers do not feed these refugees for days, or they feed them very little and badly. When they finally do eat (homemade chicken soup!), their stomachs are so empty that many cannot hold anything in. I heard more about the conditions at the immigration holding cell from this girl's mother. Too many people have told me the same stories over and over again to be making these accounts up.

Besides, my thrown up clothes are proof positive that all these women are speaking the truth…

I talked with an indigenous woman who voiced a broken Spanish, a second language for her. Her native tongue was K'iche', one of several Mayan languages spoken by the Guatemalans fleeing from the central highlands of their country. Another woman had her baby taken to the hospital in McAllen, waiting days for him to get out. She had her baby en route to freedom, she said; she started out in Honduras but delivered her baby in Guatemala. She was released from the hospital overnight, then she took off again with the newborn. She would not stay in that country of death.

Why would she remain in another violent country she did not know? The young woman just kept going. When she made it to immigration at the border, she collapsed. The guard at least rushed both mother and child to the hospital, the child dehydrated. They released the baby finally, a few days after releasing the mother to *Sacred Heart*. She was so grateful to be in a place that was taking care of her instead of shipping her out… The smile this young woman beamed as she left the center a few days later, baby against her breast, in a brand new baby pouch sling —carrying a bag filled with diapers, baby food, and clothes for the baby until she reached her own mother and father— she would never forget her stay at McAllen.

And we would never forget her.

A mother with her two sons who spoke K'iche', *one of several Mayan languages spoken by Guatemalans escaping from the central highlands of the country.*

Have we thought about what it must be like to live in a place where we would rather deliver our baby on the road, then get up and go, rather than stay the violence of living there, or having our children grow up in the vehemence of the times, go to school there, become educated in misery? Have we realized what a journey must mean to someone who speaks no English, very little Spanish, but who would rather live that, than stay in her home country, because that only means certain death? Do we realize what strength we must have to go it alone, with small children, to risk everything, to move to an unknown place in the cold north called Sioux City, Iowa? Most likely we probably don't know how to pronounce or even find the place, yet we know we would risk anything for the sake of our children…

How can we say these families are not refugees?

17

A young mother told me she was walking along the river, on a high cliff, and she saw that alligators were nearby below. Whether this was really so or imagined —what she had been told by *coyotes* [1] trying to scare her— it had worked, but not enough to stop her from going forward. She instructed her young son to keep throwing pebbles ahead of him as they walked, to keep his eyes peeled for any movement; alligators were afraid of falling rocks, she said. When mother and son were flung into the river by the smuggler who turned away —with the money they paid him in his pocket— she held on to her son and kept wading frantically on to the other side.

At the McAllen Bus Terminal, young families wait for buses to take them to their final destinations.

I've been telling these young mothers to make sure to seek a lawyer before going to their court dates. In their pack of papers, they receive a list of pro bono places where they can seek help once they get to their destinations. I don't know, though. Those places must be overwhelmed with work too ...

Still, if everyone helps out —as the folks in McAllen have been helping, as folks everywhere have been flocking to places like this embracing city— things will work out. I think, most of all, people are good and kind. Most folks want to help others; they believe in justice. And I would surmise most understand, undoubtedly, that these refugees are escaping a violence and horror we cannot even imagine.

Think, how bad can things be that a woman leaves her country, not even speaking Spanish —never mind English— because she fears for her life? How can anyone say that she wants to leave her homeland, to come to a country where she does not understand and is not understood? That she wants to take advantage of us?

These are brave women, brave children. I admire their courage, and I commend their spirit. But I also admire the brave women and men I met in McAllen, who have put aside their differences to help others in need. Because that is what good people do.

I only hope that as teachers, we can continue to do the same.

[1] A coyote is a person who smuggles Latin Americans across the US border, typically for a high fee.

IF I COME TO YOUR DOOR

By PW Covington

If I came to your door, scared and alone

Would you help me?

If I arrived in the dead of night,

With nothing but scars on my back,

Would you rip your laundry into bandages for me?

If the tears from my cheeks would fill the Rio Grande River,

The Nile River, The Jordan River;

Would my sorrows be enough

To reach you?

If I came to you, in your church,

Asking for one day of peace and freedom,

Would you prosecute me?

While praying for those sheltered within your walls?

Lost: Children of the River

If I came to you, speaking a strange tongue,

Would we laugh and smoke and dine together,

Sharing common tastes?

If I came to you,

Without bag, without horse, without cart,

Would you shoulder your rifle aimed at my heart?

To deny a hope, to rage against fate,

May be the quickest way to teach a child hate.

You have cast aside diamonds, and rubies, and teachings so wise;

Stealing the dreams from ancient, brown, eyes

Only savage nobles on la frontera today,

And nothing more

If I came to your door.

INOCENCIA INTERUMPIDA

By Raquel López Suárez

¿Quién tiene la verdad que oprime?
¿Quién el castillo que aprisiona?
su sudor se quiebra en el alba
vagando deshidratado
en el rio…en el fuego
su corazón desolado.

¿Quién tiene la verdad que oprime?
¿Quién ata la ruleta a su espalda?
la bestia anida sus sueños
el águila no espera su vuelo
acido cubriendo su cuerpo
sus plumas tiradas en el suelo.

¿Quién tiene la verdad que oprime?
¿Quién alimenta el pulmón de miedo?
el viento devora sus ojos

sus pies se comen sus gritos

se arrastra, sacuden el cielo

y la apatía…cada vez más, abraza el duelo.

¿Quién tiene la verdad que oprime?

¿Quién el delirio del poder malsano?

la ignorancia vestida de seda

la posesión del ser acusado

lágrimas negras en el sol

tortura con hilos blindados.

¿Quién tiene la verdad que oprime?

¿Quién culpa la luna por salir de noche?

clava la estaca con filo obstinado

pintados los peces de sangre

sus aletas les han cortado

su ombligo solo queda…en un derecho olvidado.

IN THE DARK, DRIFTING

By Octavio Quintanilla

If love ever climbs a canoe, rest assured
    that it will drift down stream
        until no star is bright enough
to guide it back.
It will disappear with the current,
        eventually becoming
current, wanting nothing
        more than what lies ahead.

If love ever takes a break
        from the world's desires,
        there'll come a time it'll pull
a black cloth over its head,
        unexpectedly, so as not to look
at how even the chance
of dying with dignity
is taken from us.

VIGIL

By Octavio Quintanilla

Someone is dying
far from your sleep,
        embracing a pillow,
coughing pieces
of your name.
        They have faith
you'll come to kneel
at their side,
        bring a crucifix,
a string of sunlight
between your fingers.
        Someone is dying
far from your sleep.
You embrace a pillow,
        clench their name
between your teeth.

UNACCOMPANIED MINORS

By Phyllis Wax

fifty thousand in less than a year
scarred, scared
exhausted
stomachs gnawing

to escape violence
there's no hiding from at home,
in the neck between the Americas,
surviving the trek
through endless Mexico
and now

they sleep on a warehouse floor
in Nogales
sprawled in
the myriad positions
children sleep in—
snuggled to a sibling
arm or leg
overlapping
flopped supine, mouth agape—
detainees of a resistant state

The soft sighs of their breathing

warm the cold cement they lie on

while lawmakers want to
    send in the National Guard

NEW SHOES

By Aida Escalante

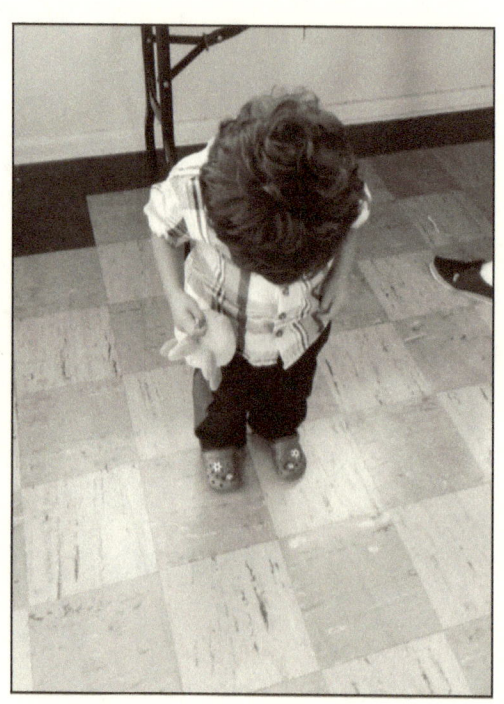

NEW SHOES AT IC CATHEDRAL

By Aida Escalante

REFUGEES

By Cesar Riojas

REFUGEES II

By Cesar Riojas

DON'T BE AFRAID GRINGO, A HONDURAN WOMAN SPEAKS FROM THE HEART: THE STORY OF ELVIA ALVARADO

By Edward Vidaurre

"We're not going to solve our problems through handouts. Until we change the system all the charity in the world won't take us out of poverty."

Almost 30 years later and I'm sending my grandchildren on la bestia to find hope. Sit on the minerals and wheat, shit on them and piss too if need to, the first gabacho you see, show him your teeth and say, these are teeth of pobreza, no de animales pendejos, not of criminals, but of dreamers, not of false refugees, but of calloused footed indios that just want fresh water and warm milk to drink and raise our children with, this hair is broken and torn beyond repair, but we want shampoo that smell of lavender and sage, these hands don't steal, look! I'll chop them off and send them sailing down the Rio Grande for your precious Catan to feast on, these eyes don't give ojo, they help reduce the drought for your blue bonnets to bloom, we are the children of the lost river, our grandma Elvia said, don't be afraid gringo, we're only coming to take a piece of what you've stolen, just a pedazo...in comparison.

UNTAMED

By Amalia L. Ortiz

The border crisis has a name. It is Cristal. Her name is Kiara.

The border crisis speaks Spanish so quickly, I am inept with my rusty tongue.

The crisis is named Kelley and has carried her son Peter all the way from Honduras.

The crisis is five years old. It is 3 years old. It is in its mid-twenties.

The crisis is two years old and learned to walk, but does not trust his own feet anymore

The crisis does not trust being outside of a mother's embrace.

The crisis needs a shower. It has been 8 days. It has been 20 days.

It has been *God-knows-how-long* since the crisis has showered.

The border crisis has tiny dreadlocks beginning to form at the nape.

At the Sacred Heart church, everyone claps when the border crisis enters.

> *Bien venidos. We welcome you.*
> *Now, tell us your name.*

Overwhelmed by the border crisis,

I try to focus on what is controllable,

like two small girls in a portable shower stall.
The sisters, Cristal and Kiara, trust so easily,
I could wet their weary feet with my tears—
bow my head and offer my hair as an unworthy washcloth...
Overwhelmed by the border crisis,
I try to focus on what is controllable—
unfit am I to even be their Mary Magdalene
No room. Many will say.
Cast stones and spit. Turn the border crisis away.
Overwhelmed by the border crisis,
I try to focus on what is controllable
like dressing the little one quickly,
so Cristal is left with some privacy and dignity.

They asked me to give you a poem.
But, what you need is a bowl of soup.
They asked me to give you a poem.
But instead, I will fit you for shoes.
They asked me to give you a poem.
But, what you need is a shower and a bed.
They asked me to give you a poem.
But instead, I will comb out your hair, and paint your tiny nails.
They asked me to give you a poem.
But, what you need is a safe home.
They asked me to give you a poem.
But, all the talking in the world is not what you need.
So instead, I will stay quiet and listen
as you tell me your name.

BORDERLAND BLOOD MOON

By Cesar D. Leon

On the night of the blood moon I drank a beer with my mother after we had a bowl of charro beans she had bought at the corner taqueria. They were salty and the cilantro had lost its bitter green punch, but they went well with the cold Bud. It had been years since she had prepared her own frijoles. It wasn't that the stove didn't work well, as she said, but the lack of helping hands that had moved away to a better life. Hands that helped clean the beans and take out the stray pebbles. Hands that helped cut the salted pork fat into slippery squares. Hands that chopped white onions and blood red tomatoes. Hands that held up steamy spoons of thick bean broth to hungry mouths while she watched. Sitting at the table she told me my beard was getting too long. She laughed when I told her I wanted to look like San Jose.

"Hoy hay luna de sangre", I said to her by the screen door before leaving. She answered, "la luna todo lo ve".

DREAMING IN NOIR: CHAPTER ONE HUNDRED FORTY-FIVE
(PARA LOS NIÑOS DE LA FRONTERA)

By Fernando Esteban Flores

Las estrellas caen

Caminando entre nosotros

La obscuridad consumiendo

La débil luz que les queda

Las horas adelgazan

El reloj cargardo del ayer

Una pistola en la sien

El amor un intento abortado

—un substituto vano—

Detiene el éxito mortal

Perdiendo más que minutos

El alma, enferma y paralitica

Tirado al lado del camino

De nuestros sueños interrumpidos

Y

Ya no vemos el camino enfrente

WHICH WAY'S HOME

By Fernando Esteban Flores

Though we leave our place
Of birth behind with empty bellies
Tired feet & little hope
Of ever seeing loved ones again
Swimming the Río Grande
Walking long stretches
Over blistering sand
Riding el tren de la muerte *La Bestia*
Or cram into trucks & trailers
Praying we make it undetected
Each paying all we have
Maybe more
El coyote says we'll be
Taken care of once we cross
Over rivers canyons deserts mountains
Where they spit on us call us aliens
Wetbacks, illegal immigrants

Undocumented
Terrorists they yell but
The only terrorists we see
Are angry men with loaded guns
Pointed at our foreheads
Not once do they say
Human beings
We lose friends children family
When it's our turn
We run *al otro lado*
& though some get through
We never arrive

FOR GILBERT RAMOS

By Joseph Ross

15 year-old Guatemalan boy who died in the Texas desert, June, 2014

Before you left, your mother
draped you with fifty Hail Marys,

a rosary of white wood,
a constellation she hoped might

guide you. But Texas does not
know these prayers. It knows

that desert air is thirsty
and you are made of water.

It drank you slowly. Your name
only linked to your body by the string

of Aves still around your neck,
the small cross pressing against your
wooden skin, the color of another cross.
You left home on May seventeenth

with one change of clothes and two
countries ahead of you, your brother's

phone number hidden on the back
of your belt buckle so the coyote

couldn't find it. The coyotes pray
in the language of extortion.

The phone number was eventually
found by a Texas official whose name

your brother couldn't remember. She called
and spoke in the language of bones. He translated

her news into "pray for us, sinners,
now and at the hour of our death."

His prayer meant "brother," a word
he kept moist, just beneath his tongue.

PUES LO QUE HA PASADO

By Sister Juliana Garcia

Allá en mi pueblito
Yo vivía contento
Alegre jugaba
Con los otros güercos.

A veces jugamos
Y también reñimos
Pero siempre al fin
Quedamos amigos.

Que's lo que ha pasado
De aquí a poco tiempo
Que somos los mismos
Y nos hemos vuelto grandes enemigos!

¿Quién es responsable?
Todos respondemos
¡El otro es el culpable!

La infancia inocente
La hemos olvidado
De cerca y de lejos
La hemos abusado.

Naciones estrujadas
Vomitan a sus hijos

Ellos buscan amparo
Ellos buscan cobijo en lugares lejanos.
Con hambre y sacrificio
Unos logran hacerla
Otros en su camino
Solo encuentran la muerte
El fin de su destino.

CHILD FROM CENTRAL AMERICA

By Brenda Riojas

CHILDREN LEFT TO WANDER

By Jenny Campos Galvan

MOTHER AND SON

By Brenda Riojas

WELCOME FLAGS

By Brenda Riojas

HISTORIA VIVIENTE

By Sister Juliana Garcia

Mujeres solas
Mujeres dejadas
No será por cierto...
Desafortunadas!

Hombres sin trabajo
Y sin esperanza
Que solo han vivido
Una vida mala.

Se echaron al raso
A ver que sacaban
Dejaron los hijos,
La esposa, la casa.

A ver si su vida
Algo mejoraba
Cruzaron desiertos,
Ríos y montañas.

Y al llegar hallaron
Una gran muralla,
Juzgar a estos hombres
Es no tener alma.

ENTRE AMIGOS

By Brenda Riojas

He thought they were joking, sus amigos
de la infancia, his childhood friends.

They played soccer in alleyways and open
fields, ate corn tortillas off the comal,
papayas fresh cut; they savored the pupusas
with queso y frijoles, washed down
with a glass of horchata;

they daydreamed in the shade about their
tomorrows. They smiled then in their El Salvador.

But their invitation arrived one day
without smiles. They came to his home,
to show him they weren't joking, left him
with broken ribs and a scar
above his right brow, a reminder he carries.

To be clear they were not joking,

his childhood friends, sus amigos

de la infancia threatened to kill

his five-year-old daughter if

he did not join them, la mara, the MS13.

He plays hide and seek now.

He tried two times to cross,

saved enough to pay the coyotes,

clutched his daughter to his chest

as he navigated waist high in river waters.

He sits across from her as she eats

her caldo de pollo at the respite center

at Sacred Heart Church in McAllen; she colors

inside the lines; her favorite colors purple and pink.

She smiles.

He wishes he could remember how.

AAAAYYY! MIS HIJOOOOOOOSSSS!

By Nephatlí De León

The night owl hears
a ghost by the river
her cries are ice daggers

she tears at her hair
the wisp of her dress
is mixed with the dew
she floats by the water
a spirit unable to rest
as long as the children come
as long as the children are lost
between cities and trains
between mountains and plains
or drowned in society's rage

she picks up the bones of the dead
some are still heavy with lead
she comforts the dying, the raped
their innocence plundered with hate

the thousands that manage to live
have traumas we cannot forgive
their perilous journey is not done
there's new men with dangerous guns
the woman goes with them to court
she weeps when they're scooped up like dung

she cries when they're huddled alone

the tired the poor, the struggling hungry masses
yearning to live and be free ...

the night owl hoots out -- wooo wooo
the beast of the road unburdens its load
hundreds and hundreds of kids by the river
no one to give them a hand, a piece of their heart
and the woman screams howls of centuries' pain
the children are soaked by a merciless rain
people can hear the ghost by the river
her cries are ice daggers that sever your heart
    Aaaayyyyy !!! Mis Hijooooooooossssss !!!

CHILDREN OF THE RIVER

By Nephatlí De León

hey
there's a bunch of kids coming !
where do they come from ?
nobody knows
where are their parents ?
nobody knows
why are they here?
nobody knows
what shall we do with them ?
nobody knows
how did they get here?
nobody knows
where did u find them ?
by the river, the river, the river …

there's 10 , there's 20
hungry and wet
skinny and dirty like dogs
there's no note in their pocket
for their teacher or their ride
there's no lunch in their bag
they got no bag
no dry or extra clothes
for their summer day in camp
no flashlight
they're shadows

they're profiles
they're non existing baggage
they're scraps

the dirty water you throw out
with the baby
like pieces of crap
they're so tired
they can't even take a nap
they could be killed
like a dog or a cat
or even violated at that

hey there's 20 more
50 half a mile away …
there's hundreds
there's a thousand
there's 60 thousand
what's going on?
why would any kid
leave their home?

what home ?
these kids got no home
they only got threats
join a gang or pay up
sell drugs, sell your body
sell your soul
to the devil or the trolls
nobody's there to care
dad left a long time ago
to America or the morgue
so did mom, brother and sis
something the cartels didn't miss
nor the local group of thugs

but all these kids need a hug
need a mother need some love
love is a four letter word
like four letters make up hate

everyone is on the take

police stations are fake
there's a line of collectors
for protection money
and a line on the collectors
or they lose their honey…

I'll tell u real
I'll tell u true
everybody knows who's who
they know back home
they know in the USA
but everybody is afraid to say
why things happen this way

it's all an American production
the worst human reduction
author of the drug cartels
finances customers, weapons
pretends to chase the bad guys
but in the end it's up to ICE
to act like it is nice
to bring buckets of ice
to despise and say you gotta go back
even if your life is under attack !

where is all this going on ?
it all starts at home
way down south side of the tracks
below the train they call the beast
where the gangs have a feast
and it ends up by the border
in drastic human disorder
where ? all these children
　　by the river the river the river…

UNTITLED

By Sister Norma Pimentel

BORDER HEADS

By Celeste De Luna

CONTRIBUTOR BIOS

Aide Escalante is a freelance photographer from Brownsville, Texas. She says, "with a camera in my hands I am seeing and finding in people's lives the bright light of hope reflected in their eyes."

She adds, "Photography has given me greater insight to people, their cultures and their beliefs. It fuels my thirst to learn more about the world and what lies beyond the camera lens."

Amalia Ortiz, Tejana poet and playwright, appeared on three seasons of Russell Simmons Presents Def Poetry on HBO. She was awarded the Alfredo Cisneros Del Moral Foundation Grant from Sandra Cisneros and a writing residency at the National Hispanic Cultural Center. She is a CantoMundo Fellow, a Hedgebrook writer-in-residence alumna, and an MFA graduate in creative writing at The University of Texas - Pan American. In 2015, Wings Press published her first collection of poetry, *Rant. Chant. Chisme.*

Ana M. Fores Tamayo is a doctoral candidate in Comparative Literature from New York University. She never completed her PhD because motherhood got in the way. Switching fields from publishing, she went back to academia, only to find the Ivory Tower inhospitable. Soon she was fighting for adjunct faculty like her. She began a petition, which presently holds over 10,000 signatures. Fores Tamayo's work now centers around DREAMers, undocumented students, but most importantly, refugee children and their families.

Brenda Nettles Riojas is a CantoMundo Fellow. She is the host of Corazón Bilingüe, a weekly radio program that addresses the dynamics of language and culture. She is also the editor of The Valley Catholic newspaper. Brenda earned her M.F.A. from the University of New Orleans. Her first collection of Spanish poems – "La Primera Voz Que Oí". She co-edited "Writing to Be Heard / Escúchame: Voices from the Chicho" with Alan Oak.

Celeste De Luna: "My work is sometimes disturbing. The confluence of American and Xicano culture clash and sometimes harmonize in my work. My seemingly morbid interests go well with the death and despair of the border experience. Common themes in my work include migrant/border experiences of women, children, and families, the social effects of documentation status, and the spiritual struggle of conflicting identities, including "survivor's guilt".

Celeste De Luna is a painter/printmaker from Harlingen, Texas. She has exhibited her work in various cities in the Rio Grande Valley, San Antonio, San Diego, and Chicago. You can reach her at delunaceleste@gmail.com and see more of her work at www.celestedeluna.com.

César De León has called El Valle home for the past 30plus years. His poetry has been published in various anthologies including Juventud: Growing Up on the Border and Along the River 2, as well as in various journals.

Cesar Riojas, Jr. has been taking photos for more than 30 years. When he's not helping companies implement process optimization and operational excellence systems, he is behind the camera. The camera and his travels around the world have focused his lens on people, places and the stories they tell. He freelances regularly for The Valley Catholic newspaper, and has received awards for this work from the Catholic Press Association.

Christopher Carmona is a Chican@ Beat poet from the Rio Grande Valley of South Texas. The Texas Observer recognized him as being one of the top five writers in 2014. He has two books of poetry, beat and I Have Always Been Here. He edited The Beatest State In The Union: An Anthology of Beat Texas Writings with Chuck Taylor and Rob Johnson, and completed Nuev@s Voces Poeticas: A Dialogue about New Chican@ Poetics with Isaac Chavarría, Gabriel Sanchez, & Rossy Lima Padilla published by Slough Press in 2015. Currently he is the organizer of the Annual Beat Poetry and Arts Festival and the Artistic Director of the Coalition of New Chican@ Artists.

Edward Vidaurre is the author of four books. I Took My Barrio On A Road Trip, (Slough Press 2013), Insomnia (El Zarape Press 2014), Beautiful Scars: Elegiac Beat Poems (El Zarape Press 2015), and his latest collection Chicano Blood Transfusion (FlowerSong Books) was published this year. Vidaurre is the founder of Pasta, Poetry, and Vino--a monthly open mic gathering of artists, poets, and musicians. He resides in McAllen, TX with his wife and daughter.

Fernando Esteban Flores: I am a native Texan residing in San Antonio, graduated from the University of Texas at Austin with a Bachelor of Arts in English and have taught writing at various San Antonio secondary schools.

Isis Hinojosa: Escritora y pintora autodidacta, PINTORA ARTISTICA, y Creadora en Arte Visual at ISIS ARTE Y PINTURA (Facebook page).

Jenny Campos Galvan is a visual artist from New Orleans, Louisiana. She is a first generation American, born of Ecuadorian mother and Guatemalan father. Her piece "Children left to wander" speaks to the unanswerable question only these children really understand and are left to fully face. Original is watercolor and ink on 10.5" × 14.5" watercolor paper.

Jose G. Cano is a painter, song-writer, and well-rounded artista from the Mexico-U.S. frontera/border región in Texas.

Joseph Ross is a writer hailing from Washington, D.C. His first book of poetry *MEETING BONE MAN* is available from Main Street Rag Publishing. You can order it for a discount at http://mainstreetrag.com/bookstore/product-tag/joseph-ross/

His second book of poetry, *GOSPEL OF DUST* is available from Main Street Rag Publishing at http://mainstreetrag.com/bookstore/product-tag/joseph-ross/ It was released June 18, 2013.

Sister Juliana García, a native of Toledo, Spain, was founder of the Missionaries of Jesus, a religious community dedicated to serving the people of the Rio Grande Valley and Matamoros. She died Nov. 17, 2014 at the age of 81. She was the director of Casa Oscar Romero in the 1980s, a shelter that housed thousands of Central American refugees seeking political asylum in the United States. She also initiated the jail ministry in detention centers across the Rio Grande Valley.

Norma Pimentel is a sister with the Missionaries of Jesus and executive director of Catholic Charities of the Rio Grande Valley, the charitable arm of the Diocese of Brownsville, providing oversight of different ministries and programs in the areas of emergency assistance. She leads efforts in the community that respond to emergency relief in times of disaster and crisis in the Rio Grande Valley. In the summer of 2014, she launched the humanitarian outreach for refugees from Central America.

Octavio Quintanilla's work has appeared in *Salamander, RHINO, Alaska Quarterly Review, Southwestern American Literature, The Texas Observer, Texas Books in Review,* and elsewhere. He is a CantoMundo Fellow and holds a PhD from the University of North Texas. Currently, he teaches Literature and Creative Writing in the MA/MFA program at Our Lady of the Lake University. He is a regular interviews contributor to *Voices de La Luna: A Quarterly Poetry and Arts Magazine* and author of the poetry collection, *If I Go Missing* (Slough Press, 2014).

Phyllis Wax writes in Milwaukee on a bluff overlooking Lake Michigan. Her poetry has appeared in *Ars Medica, Verse Wisconsin, Your Daily Poem, The New Verse News, Naugatuck River Review, Wisconsin Poets' Calendar* as well as other journals and anthologies, both print and online. Social issues inspire much of her work.

PW Covington has been a fixture in the spoken word and Indie Lit community of Texas for nearly 20 years. As an 18 year old Air Transportation troop in the USAF, he deployed to Mogadishu, Somalia to deliver aid to and protect those victimized by that region's violent refugee crisis and famine. He has remained active in disaster relief and recovery work ever since. He has lived for periods of time in the Copper Canyon region of Mexico, and believes that bridges are better than fences.

Covington's newly released novel is titled "Dear Elsa,"

Raquel López Suárez. Originaria de la ciudad de Río Bravo, Tam. Méx. Titulada en Pedagogía a nivel primaria y medio superior (UPN, 2002-2006). Actualmente es residente de los Estados Unidos de América. Graduada de Project Ignite (PLP, TX 2009-2011) donde adquirió conocimientos en diversas áreas, tales como; escritura creativa, poesía, teatro, business management, toastmasters, promotora de salud, etc. En el 2011 se inició en los estudios de teología y psicoterapia (The Ecumenical Center for Religion and Health, Campus McAllen, TX). Autora del libro de pensamientos, reflexiones y poesía, "Lluvias Acarameladas" (Palibrio, 2013). Fundadora/directora del foro de expresión literario-artístico "Enero Rojo Lunar" (RGV, 2014-2016) incluyendo talentos de USA y de México. Ha participado con sus textos en diversos programas literarios, festivales, instituciones sociales y comunitarias de algunas ciudades del sur del Valle de Texas y del norte de Tamaulipas, MX. (2010-2016).

ABOUT THE EDITORS

Gabriel H. Sanchez is a publisher, writer, and poet from the Rio Grande Valley in South Texas. He is also an actor, theatre director, filmmaker, and entrepreneur.

Isaac Chavarría still lives in Alton, TX and is currently working on his second manuscript of poetry, *Moxado*. His first poetry collection, *Poxo*, won the 2014 NACCS Tejas Poetry Prize.

Contact & Orders: theravingpress@gmail.com

Website: www.theravingpress.com

www.ingramcontent.com/pod-product-compliance
Lightning Source LLC
Chambersburg PA
CBHW020649250626
47154CB00008B/2881